THE
NEW YORKER
TWENTY-FIFTH ANNIVERSARY
ALBUM

THE NEW YORKER

TWENTY-FIFTH ANNIVERSARY

ALBUM

1925   1950

HARPER COLOPHON BOOKS

HARPER & ROW, PUBLISHERS

NEW YORK, HAGERSTOWN, SAN FRANCISCO, LONDON

This edition appears by arrangement with *The New Yorker*.

First HARPER COLOPHON edition published 1977

STANDARD BOOK NUMBER: 06–090553–0

79 80 81 5 4 3 2

Lithographed in the United States by
The Murray Printing Company, Forge Village, Mass.

Design and layout by Carmin Peppe, of The New Yorker staff.

FOREWORD

The drawings in this book were chosen from among the more than twenty thousand published in The New Yorker since its first issue, in 1925. To help you find your way around, the pictures presented here are more or less chronologically arranged in five sections:

The Late Twenties
The Early Thirties
The Late Thirties
The Early Forties
The Late Forties

...the late twenties...

"Economy Is Idealism in Its Most Practical Form."

"Couldn't you let that skirt down a little, Mary Louise? It's only an inch below your garters."

"For heaven's sake, mother! Do you want me to look like a monk?"

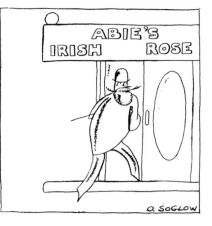

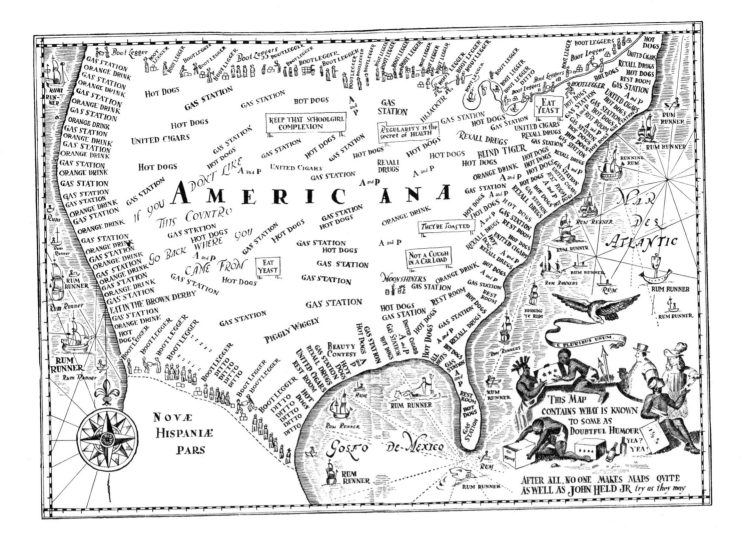

"*Quick, mama—look! President Coolidge!*"

"*Oh Goody! Douglas Fairbanks is showing tonight at the Teatro Romano.*"

"It's broccoli, dear."
"I say it's spinach, and I say the hell with it."

"Oop—sorry."

"THE GREEN HAT"

Miss Cornell's Latest and Mr. Arlen's
First Triumph in the Theatre

The talented Miss Katherine Cornell, the Iris March of the stage version of "The Green Hat," and Mr. Michael Arlen (né Kouyoumdjian), its author, stop to consider things between acts.

At latest reports, the line at the box office reached from the Broadhurst Theatre to the Battery, with Miss Gertrude Ederle treading water in the Bay. Mr. Arlen is thus repeating the magnificent clean-up that he made in Chicago and Detroit. "The Green Hat" is full of the most delicious pathological and obstetrical conversation for those who never have any fun at home.—R. B.

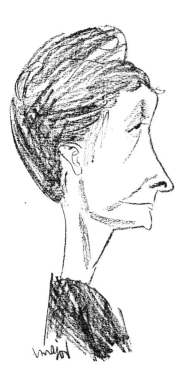

Georgia O'Keeffe

'TWAS CHRISTMAS IN THE PEST HOUSE.

"They're discussing sex—isn't that cute?"

"Yeah, once break the ice wit' Joisey this way and there's no tellin' what'll happen."

JAMES J. WALKER—*Who was practically elected last week when E. H. Wilson, chairman of the research committee of the Kings County Republican Advisory Committee, published the fact that the Citizens Union record showed that Senator Walker had, in 1912, introduced bills in the Legislature increasing the time during which liquor saloons might be open.*

ADVERTISING COPY WRITER (*reflectively*): *"Grace, poise, charm, and—ah—floatability."*

THE TOMATO SURPRISE

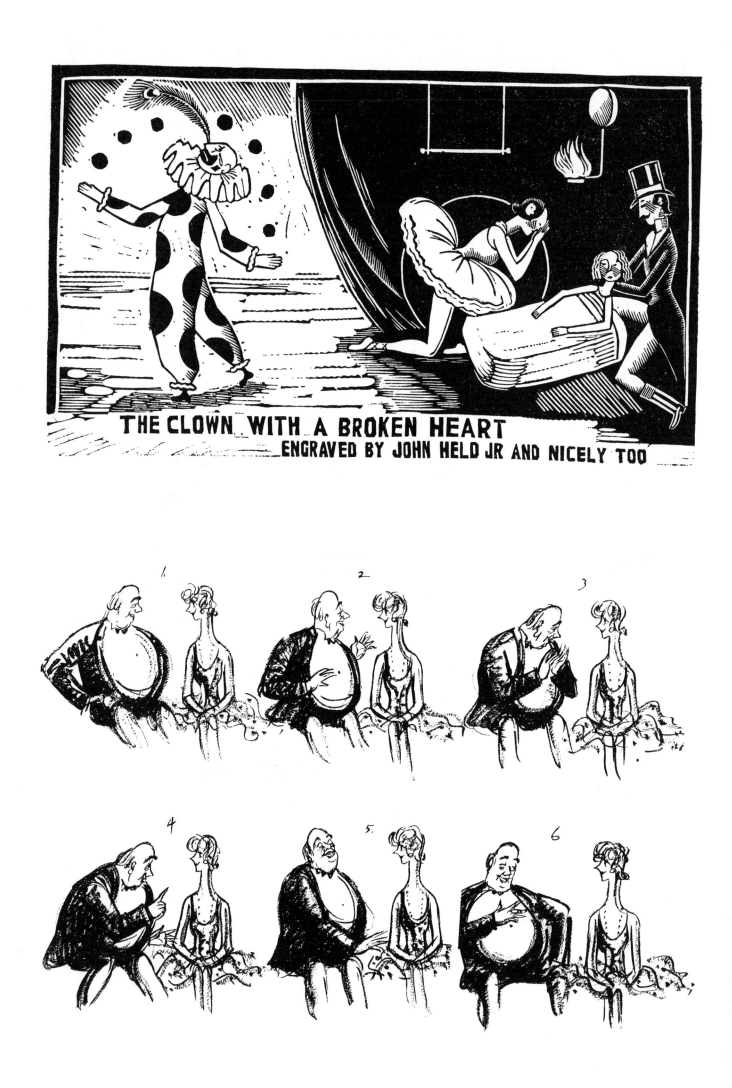

THE CLOWN WITH A BROKEN HEART
ENGRAVED BY JOHN HELD JR AND NICELY TOO

THE DOORMAN WHO FORGOT THE NAME OF THE OLDEST MEMBER

"You're a very intelligent little woman, my dear."

"No, I have to stay here
and work. I'm unloading copper."

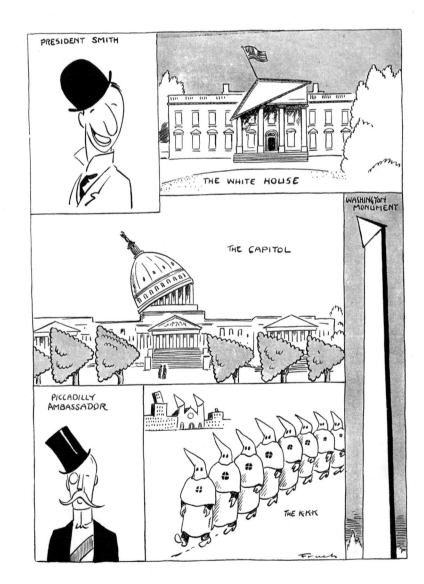

"Smart-lookin' gentleman,
weren't he?"
"Which one, sweetheart?"
"The one I jus' tripped up."
"Whoops! Ain't you the sly
croquette—steady!"

POSSIBLE INFLUENCE OF AL SMITH
ON THE NATIONAL CAPITAL

SOLVING THE PARKING PROBLEM

MOE SMITH AND IZZY EINSTEIN—Who lost their jobs as prohibition agents last week and who, we can't help thinking, ought to make the best pair of bootleggers in these parts, knowing what they do about the sources of supply. They are here pictured in the disguises in which they evaded detection in the night clubs of New York.

THE SORT OF THING THAT BRINGS JOY TO THE ASHMAN'S BLACK HEART

A WHOLE, NICE, NEW, BIG, TWENTY-STORY, CO-OPERATIVE APARTMENT HOUSE TO WAKE UP
AT SIX IN THE MORNING

"I'm gonna show me profile, dearie!"

"Profile? Whoops—I ain't even takin' me coat off!"

"DIAMOND LIL"

This is Mae West herself as the lovely Queen of the Bowery in the rowdy play at the Royale. Her glorification amidst all the whoopee and carryings on becomes, Heaven knows just why, a thing one should not miss.

The Fatal Night in De Russey's Lane

"Having a good time?"
"Heavenly!"

The Rise and Fall of Man

Primate   **Neanderthal Man**   **Socrates**   **W. J. Bryan**

"How do you like Vassar, Annabelle?"
"Well, it's just so juvenile and childish I'm _almost_ passing out."

THE NEW YORKER'S LATE FALL AND WINTER SHOWING
OF CARTOONS TO THE TRADE

With every confidence of favorable reception, The New Yorker takes pleasure in exhibiting to the press of the nation its regular seasonal showing of cartoons. It has been our privilege to supply such original drawings on standard themes for many years, and we bring forward this offering of something new in old friends with every confidence of favorable reception. The present set of drawings may be had at the usual low cost and, to customers taking the entire lot, we will include a handsome print of "The Good Samaritan." The New Yorker takes a pardonable pride in its record of many years of faithful service, and is happy to announce that its staff of artists is already at work upon its late Winter offerings.

First again! With its usual promptness and initiative, The New Yorker is able to take pride in being the first to display the newest line of cartoon illustrations to the Daily Press. Reproduction rights to any of the cartoons here shown may be had at The New Yorker's regular low price of ten cents each, or the entire lot for fifteen cents. A testimonial signed, "A satisfied customer for ten years" (believed to be the Literary Digest) says: "Your service has given complete satisfaction. We have found the cartoons regulation and good upon practically all occasions." The New Yorker takes pleasure, too, in announcing that our late-fall-and-winter line will be available in due time, offering a comprehensive treatment of the standard subjects—the Pilgrim and the Turkey, the Precious Lump of Coal, Father Winter, etc.

THE GENIAL HOST: *"Well, ol' top, there's the alcohol, citric acid, glycerine, oil of juniper, essence of orange, oil of coriander, distilled water, and an empty gin bottle. Mix it to suit yourself."*

OTTO H. KAHN—From whom all blessings flow. Forty-seven conductors of jazz bands, seventeen theatrical producers and the entire staff of the Metropolitan Opera House began talking of their artistic aims and ideals when he mysteriously bought a plot of land in Fifty-seventh Street the other day.

"Yes, Mattie, I'd trust my little girl anywhere."
"Well, Mother, I like that!"

"Lafayette, we are here."

"Listen, Basil, I'm at 125th Street—what ought I to do?"

"Oh, Al Smith's all right, but I'm fer leaving prosperity alone."

"I'm sure of the L and I'm almost sure of the P. Should I go on?"

"Bill, we got mice!"

"No, Joe, Jock's father was Payne Whitney."

O. SOGLOW

THE REV. FRANCIS P. DUFFY—Who is one of the reasons that Christianity and the Catholic Church have lasted as long as they have and who celebrated his twenty-fifth anniversary as an army chaplain and his tenth as chaplain of the 69th Regiment last week.

"But you can't just ignore Humanism."

"Good night, Mrs. Parker. It's been perfectly charming."

"He has no right to look so dumb. He isn't so terribly rich."

FRANKLIN P. ADAMS—
Who, after having masqueraded
for years as the ugly duckling of
journalism, has blossomed forth
in a dashing moustache which re-
veals him as the handsome
Rajah who owns the great ruby
that was stolen from the eye of
an idol. New York's "Mr. A."

1. Very likely a gentleman will say to you some evening — "I wonder how you'd look with your hair long."

2. So you begin to ignore the barber —

5. No matter how cautiously you go about

You can't escape your dear friends — "Say, are you letting your hair grow?"

6.

Nor time to bu one milli

10. and of course you can't wear any of your hats —

11. and the dear friends ke on "Are you still letting your hair grow

3

But just as you are enjoying your new
edom you will meet a friend —

4.

"For heavens sake! what's
the matter with your hair?"

8.

es the
et, and
rpins

(For unfortunately they have a
way of falling out.)

9.

And you will probably
buy a switch — but
nothing will come of it.

12.

But the final blow comes after
ix months — "Do you know, I believe I
ike you better with your hair short."

13.

Helen E. Hokinson

well — have a
nice haircut!

"*You think I got nothin' to do tonight except argue about gettin' in this joint?*"

"*I've heard they make perfectly devoted servants.*"

"*Red Rover, Red Rover, let Professor Sturges come over!*"

Jack Dempsey

"Artistic, ain't it?"
"Yeh—but it's good."

"And
you,
Lily—tell me,
are you happy?"

"Ah—Meester Whalen?"

"Oh, she's _very_ attractive. I don't like _her_ at all."

"Waiter."

"Why Henry Whipple, I thought you were still in medical college!"

"*By Jove, Belasco must be aboard!*"

THE VICAR'S REMORSE

Having blessed the foxhounds in accordance with tradition, he feels the prick of conscience

AMERICANA SERIES

"NOW IZE DRAMPA"
ENG. BY JOHN HELD JR. WITH A SLIGHT TOUCH OF NAUSEA

The chess player and the French pastry

J. KLEIN

SEE YOURSELF AS OTHERS SEE YOU

1 2 3

"Boarda Ejicashun speakin' . . . "

YE PINK COCKATOO

"I would have given myself freely to Walt Whitman."

"His father wants him to be a lawyer, but I want him to go into a bank. It's always so nice and cool in a bank."

"Now can you hear me—you boys in the back?"

THE NEW JAZZ—WHICH IS
JUST LIKE MUSIC

...the early thirties...

A brokerage house receives an order to buy ten shares of Goldman Sachs

"Wilfred, what did I tell you about letting me drink!"

"ANIMAL CRACKERS"

The superbly turned out gentleman pictured above is the Marx called Harpo, the silent one of that remarkable family of clowns whose current idiocies are on exhibition at the Forty-fourth Street Theatre.

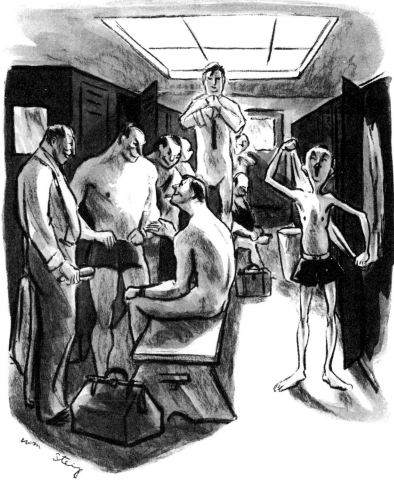

"Oh, Mademoiselle from Armenteers."

"Last one in is a purple cow!"

BREAD LINE   REGINALD MARSH

INDUSTRIAL CRISES

The day a cake of soap sank at Procter & Gamble's

"*Good Lord! Here comes that impossible yak again!*"

"*To the Gods—to the Fates—to the Rulers of Men and their Destinies . . .*"

"You're fired!"

"Well, so long. I'll see you at lunch at the Bankers Club."

"They have your eyes, but their father's hair."

"I'm so glad you like it, darling."

"Avez-vous 'Ulysses'?"

"Seventy dollars a case—and I handle only real stuff."

"Good ny-ut . . . good ny-ut, dar-ling, sleep ty-ut. . . . Don't interrupt us, operator—we're toking."

"But darling, this __is__ a ship."

HISTORICAL INCIDENTS

The Serpent watched the first of men.
There was no Eve in Eden then.

The Serpent heard him curse his fate
Because he could not find a mate.

The Serpent smiled. And by his side
That evening Adam found a bride.

"You've come? But whence?" . . . Eve told a fib.
She said that she was Adam's rib.

Could this, he wondered, be a fact?
He felt his ribs. They were intact.

So were the cat's, he found; the hare's,
The parrot's, and the polar bear's.

He knew that he was made of clay.
What Eve might be, he couldn't say.

He loved her—she was all he had—
But her deception made him sad.

Then, late one day, with startled eye
He saw a friend of Eve's go by.

And as that friend went writhing on
'Twas plain to see its ribs were gone.

Yet Adam hated to believe
It was the Serpent fathered Eve.

Here is Launcelot, cap-a-pie,
Giving Arthur's wife the eye.
Here is Arthur, from his prison,
Watching Launcelot enter his'n.

Here's a Tristan on the ocean
  Being brought up with a jerk.
He has found the magic potion
  Doesn't work.

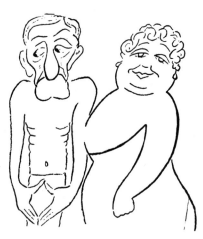

Oh, why did you marry sweet Alice, Ben Bolt,
  Who trembled, when young, at your frown?
Now it's you who are sighing, and not with delight.
  Your Alice is wearing you down.
                              —CLARENCE DAY

"Why should I dress up to see a show about a sea gull?"

"They haven't got a single tenant on the fifty-fourth floor yet, Mr. Chrysler."

"Shut your eyes, Edith— here comes another fence!"

BODY AND SOUL

"It's passed all the tests for coolness, kindness, mildness, and freshness. Now if there was only some way we could keep it from tasting lousy."

"It's Parkins, sir; we're 'aving a bit of a time below stairs."

"Roger, look at the birdie!"

"Hey, is Frank up there?"
"Wait and I'll look and see."

"Mrs. Cox,
this is my
first-born."

"*Now if Jimmie boy doesn't try to steal this next scene,
Yvonne will buy him a great big ice-cream cone.*"

"You are a
police officer,
are you not?"

"Is this the road
to Cold Spring Harbor? Answer yes or no!"

"All right, have it your way—you heard a seal bark!"

"Of course he's the son of
a Morgan partner, but then who isn't?"

"I merely wanted to tell Mr. Insull that
he's not the only one who lost his pants in
Middle West Utilities."

"I haven't taken any interest in politics
since Jimmy Walker retired."

"Take a letter to the New York Athletic Club."

SMALL FRY

Spring—and that strange pounding
in the breast

Just around the corner

THE SALOON MUST GO!

"Now see here, Ira! You paid for the trip to Chinatown!"

"Saks-Fifth Avenue. Good morning."

"Of course, in a way, Bertrand Russell is responsible for me."

JOIN THE NAVY AND SEE THE WORLD

"If we could only have one of those good old ticker-tape and paper-shower parades to take their minds off things."

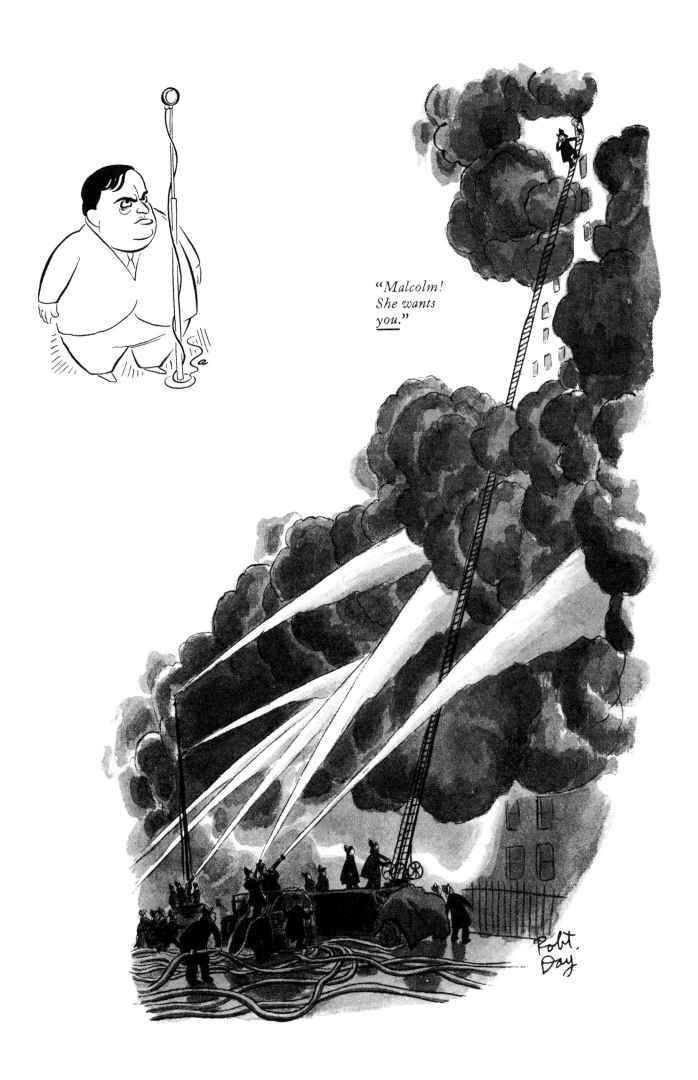

"Malcolm! She wants you."

"Do you think I like to steal?"

"Awfully nice of you to ask me to stay."

"*No, that was Lincoln we worked on last year, Ed. I never forget a face.*"

Walter Damrosch

UNLOOKED~FOR EVENT OF THE LITERARY SEASON

The Messrs. Houghton and Mifflin tender a tea to one of their authors

THE 1930'S

Breakfast

"That's your father, Horace. He perished in a stampede in Gimbel's basement."

"She's been this way ever since she saw 'Camille.'"

"Well, it's a catwalk, ain't it?"

"Lucky for you I'm not wearing a belt!"

"Here you are, folks. Are
you interested in recapturing
the glamour of a vanished era?"

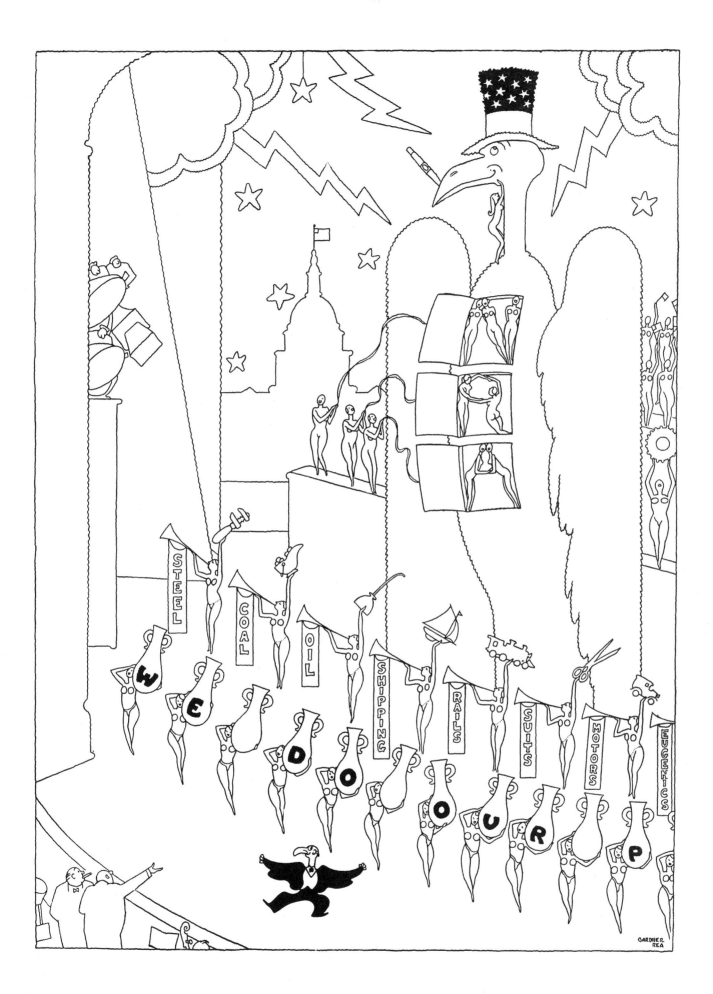

"There, Morris! If that don't bring prosperity, nothing will."

"Rose Pelswick, John S. Cohen, Mordaunt Hall, Irene Thirer, and Percy Hammond raved about the picture, but he says it smells."

"Hello, Governor Roosevelt. You haven't got a good idea for a Thanksgiving proclamation, have you?"

DREAM GIRLS of a DIM DECADE
SEVEN SUTHERLAND SISTERS
ENG. BY JOHN HELD JR SINGER OF OLD SONGS

"I've doped it out this way—the world's a stage and we're the actors, see? You, me, Mr. Hirsch— all of us. Get what I mean?"

"Best two falls out of three, Mr. Montague? Okay?"

"Very clever, sir. Brilliant satire."

"I used to bet my husband I'd die before he did—and I lost!"

"Well, well, speak of the devil—"

"Herman! Sparks is comin' outa my head!"

"Hey, what about dames?"

"Why, Mr. Trimble! I thought you were still employed at the bank!"

Jascha Heifetz

"Touché!"

"This doesn't commit us to anything, does it?"

"Dear Dorothy Dix:
I find myself in a somewhat peculiar situation."

"SIMPLE SIMON"

For those of our readers who were born during the past week, we will explain that the above is a picture of Ed Wynn, one of America's most prominent hat-wearers, now roaming about in the woods at the Ziegfeld Theatre.

"It's her third husband and
fifth baby, or maybe it's her fifth husband
and third baby. Anyway, she's in the hospital."

*"I'm not sure,
but I think he's from the Yale Psychological School."*

*"This is a hell of a time for you
to get chicken pox."*

*"I don't like his
holier-than-thou attitude."*

Toes

Worm

The boiling pot

SMALL FRY
PHENOMENA

Lightning

What makes it go?

"Boo!"

"...and we've
got wind resistance
just about licked."

"This is her first lynching."

"I feel graceful as all hell today."

"Then I wrote him an awfully nasty letter, but, you know, cute."

"Startin' kinda early, ain't we?"

"Skee dooten doo, skee dooten doo, wuday wuddy woo, wuddy wuddy woo, hey hey-eee."

"Ready or not, here I come!"

"Loser christens the Flaherty twins."

"Everything considered, he preaches a
remarkably good sermon. It's so hard
to avoid offending people like us."

"If you _really_ cared for me,
you'd take me some place where they sell gin."

*"On the right,
ladies and gentlemen,
is Bird Rock."*

Robt.
Day

"Don't just stand there—get witnesses!"

Alan Dunn

"Some fine day, my son, all this will be yours."

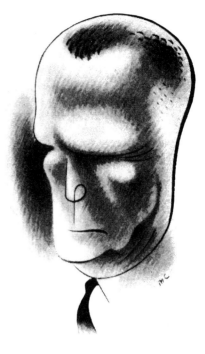

Joseph Medill Patterson

"Speak, Mr. Pennywhistle! Speak to me!"

SMALL FRY

"Indian Lament"

The RED HOT PAST
THE SOUVENIR GARTER WITH THE WITTY MOTTO
ENGRAVED BY **JOHN HELD JR** WHO IS ALWAYS UP TO SOME MISCHIEF

Capture of three physics professors

Rout

Women's G. H. Q.

Surrender

"Now the faun lies wounded, and a little wind springs up in the trees."

"For a while I toyed with architecture, but of course il faut manger—you know, it is necessary to eat."

"Silly woman! What have you done?"

"When will it ever end, Miss Hartley? When will it ever end?"

SCENES FROM THE MESOZOIC

Age after age, some old roué,
The Casanova of his day,
Delights in telling guileless lads
His oily, amorous escapades.

Sometimes a beast would learn to brood
And cultivate an awesome mood,
Or moan in quite a striking way.
This brought him fame. It does today.

Even on mesozoic beaches
There were inane though joyous screeches.

What can it be about a shore
That has always made a bather roar?
—CLARENCE DAY

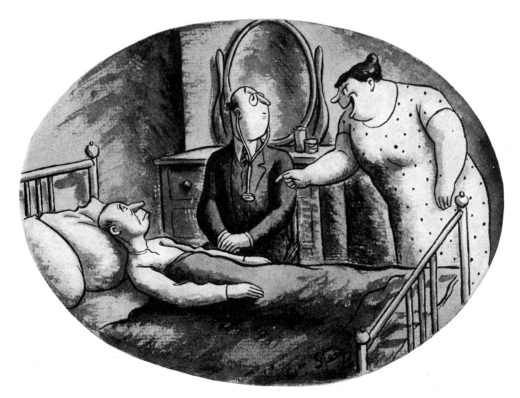

"You see,
wise guy? Grippe,
just like I told you!"

"I'm afraid this isn't much fun for you, Mr. Ewing."

"Pants? Certainly, Madam. For the little fellow?"

"See here, Pritchard, you're falling behind."

"Things still look pretty fuzzy."

"I don't care what you say—I'm cold!"

"I sing you now song in Japanese
language, but I warn you it is very, very filthy."

"That's right, stupid—
drop 'em all over the lot!"

"Here's a study for you, Doctor—he faints."

"No sense of humor? Oh, Mrs. Donahue!"

"He's very much at ease in the pulpit too."

"*Little things mean a lot to a girl, Mr. Goldsmith—like your coming to see me this way when you're cold sober.*"

"I hope you get something, darling."

"You're one of the lucky few who
have a normal skin."

"How many apostrophes in 'fo'c's'le'?"

"Of course, we must draw some sort of distinction between wishing to overthrow the government and not liking the present administration."

"Funny. I was under the impression that we had _seven_ converts."

"The CWA has commissioned me to
paint a mural here."

"I name thee Mt. Buzzie Dall!"

"Meow."

Glenn Cunningham

OUR MODERN GALLERY OF ANCIENT FAVORITES
Rape of the Sabines

"Good Lord,
I thought
you'd gone
to lunch!"

"If you can keep a secret,
I'll tell you how my husband died."

"Oh, she's been acting that way
all day. Someone told her she looks like Katharine Hepburn."

"She never discusses her age, but I know
she has her second teeth."

"What's wrong wit' oatmeal, if I ain't
bein' too inquisitive?"

"*I'm sorry, Sigmund. You frighten me, but that isn't enough for marriage.*"

"... and a box of old-fashioned wooden matches that you can strike on the seat of your pants."

"You are trustworthy, loyal, helpful, friendly, courteous, kind, obedient, cheerful, thrifty, brave, clean, reverent."

1.

2.

3.

4.

5.

6.

"You'd think George and Ella would try to patch things up for the children's sake."

"What do you want
to be inscrutable _for_, Marcia?"

"All out
for the
sack race,
Mr. McQuade."

"My man don't
wrestle till we hear it talk."

"The moon has something to do
with it. Lately he's been rising and falling with the tide."

"Look! There's that mirage again!"

"From here on they call me Squire."

"There goes Henderson following the line of least resistance again."

"Pardon me, Madame, is Cook's this way?"

*"Are you the lady
who advertised for a companion?"*

"All right, men, break step."

"Remember now, you got the brains."

"Somehow, I don't quite trust that new fellow."

"Tu wit! Tu woo! Has everybody marshmallows?"

"And Mrs. Wilkins' baby—how is _she_?"

"How beautifully the sun catches the gold
in your beard, Mr. Travilla."

"Oh, it's all very simple. Our little group simply
seize the powerhouses and the radio stations."

Dexter Fellows

"He just bought all we had and gave them their freedom."

"I told him there are some things
I won't do, and going to museums is one of them."

SMALL FRY

Danseuse

"Stop acting so innocent,
Craddock! You know very well _what_ signals."

" If my calculations are correct, you will soon
be playing third base for the Detroit Tigers."

"*I must confess I feel somewhat like a bull in a china shop.*"

"*Levering, how long have you been with us?*"

"Pombo learn things fast, eh, doctor?"

"Now look, everybody! This is the one
that cost fifty cents!"

"Boy, have they got your number!"

"*I never told her about the depression. She would have worried.*"

...the late thirties...

"Come along. We're going to the Trans-Lux to hiss Roosevelt."

"Where in Heaven's name do you think you're going?"

AN ACME
10 – 25 – 1.00
STORE WILL
BE OPENED
HERE

ACME WILL PROBABLY BE UNFAIR

"All right, Haskens, now whistle
and say, 'Are there any more at home like you?'"

"I assume, then, that you regard yourself
as omniscient. If I am wrong, correct me!"

"You certainly
have a peculiar sense of humor."

"Here comes the mother,
ladies and gentlemen—
and, boy, is
she burned up
about something!"

"Meridian 7-1212."

"All right, boys—break it up!"

"Your mother's been having a job holding him here."

"Never mind, Mrs.
Mainwaring. We'll take the will for the deed."

"Rotten shame that cheetah making off with Sir Roger's dinner jacket."

"I imagine it's the University of Southern California."

"My dear, perhaps you had better look over this ending. I don't want to be guilty of too much levity."

"Why, it seems to be all right. I don't think it's too funny—not at all."

"We'll have to go around
the Horn. They won't take a check."

A REVISED STATUARY
FOR THE CITY OF TOMORROW

"HOT~CHA!"

Mr. Bert Lahr in exact proportion to the rest of the show
at the Ziegfeld, including Miss Lupe Velez, who works
very hard, down in the lower right-hand corner.

"I'll wait for him one more year. I keep telling myself he may
be having engine trouble somewhere."

"Here's the guest room. Just make yourselves at home."

"Why, Herbie! You're _good!_"

Sonja Henie

"Here's <u>one</u> family, Mr. Gillis, that goes right through the winter without catching cold."

college work wi.. no grade below
. was elected to Sigma Delta Chi, honorary
journalism fraternity. I have also been ma-
joring in Elizabethan drama, and in my junior
year, I was editor of our college literary
monthly.

I should, therefore, appreciate hearing
from you regarding any openings you may have
on your reportorial staff, especially in your
dramatic department. I stand ready to depart
for New York on a few hours notice, in the
event of a favorable reply.

Thanking you for any consideration you may
give this application, I remain,

Sincerely yo

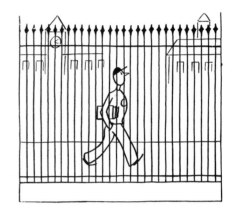

"Approach, women of Athens!"

"Well, well! The Mayor's
Reception Committee!"

"I'm barefoot."

"Professor Furbush has been telling me about the N'gambi
fertility rites—and guess what they turn out to be!"

Gargantua the Great

LIMERICKS LONG AFTER LEAR

A susceptible senior at Vassar
Is knitting an antimacassar
　　To lure her professor
　　To love and caress her,
And possibly even to pass her.

"You mean __nobody__ took any pictures?"

Brenda Diana Duff Frazier

"It's a naive domestic Burgundy without
any breeding, but I think you'll be amused by its presumption."

"Tira, I love you."

"*It was a three-alarm fire—practically gutted the place.*"

A DAY AT THE OFFICE

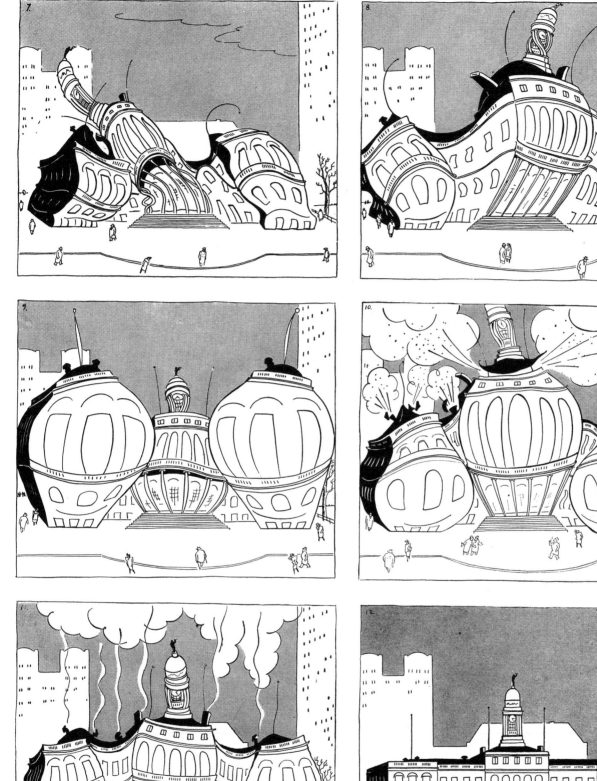

"Tell 'em to dump their industrials. Further details later."

"Congratulations, sir. You've hit the jack pot."

"Boy! Looka the sheik!"

" . . . and thanks, God, for bringing Mr. Bowers back to the Ocean House."

OUR MODERN GALLERY OF ANCIENT FAVORITES

Ulysses and the Sirens

Dispensation

Shelter

Dry Socks

Die-Hards

"I never got a
chance to return to the scene of the crime."

Eddie Arcaro

"Say, Donovan, do we have one with muffled oars?"

LITERARY RENEGADES

The Kathleen Norris Heroine Who Didn't Wait for Mr. Right

"*Most successful suit sale we ever had, I should say*"

"*You're mine! Do you understand? Mine! Mine!*"

"*Don't you think you've made Mother Squirrel just a little too much the old-fashioned parent, Mrs. Mason?*"

FAMOUS POEMS ILLUSTRATED

IV. *"Locksley Hall,"*
by Alfred, Lord Tennyson

Comrades, leave me here a little, while as yet 'tis early morn;
Leave me here, and when you want me, sound upon the bugle horn.

'Tis the place, and all around it, as of old, the curlews call,
Dreary gleams about the moorland, flying over Locksley Hall.

In the spring a livelier iris changes on the burnished dove;
In the spring a young man's fancy lightly turns to thoughts of love.

O my cousin, shallow-hearted! O, my Amy, mine no more!
O the dreary, dreary moorland! O the barren, barren shore!

Is it well to wish thee happy?—having known me; to decline
On a range of lower feelings and a narrower heart than mine!

As the husband is, the wife is; thou art mated with a clown,
And the grossness of his nature will have weight to drag thee down.

Like a dog, he hunts in dreams; and thou art staring at the wall,
Where the dying night-lamp flickers, and the shadows rise and fall.

Then a hand shall pass before thee, pointing to his drunken sleep,
To thy widowed marriage-pillows, to the tears that thou wilt weep.

Hark! my merry comrades call me, sounding on the bugle-horn,—
They to whom my foolish passion were a target for their scorn.

. . . I will take some savage woman, she shall rear my dusky race.

Iron-jointed, supple-sinewed, they shall dive, and they shall run,
Catch the wild goat by the hair, and hurl their lances in the sun.

"*Madam, Mr. Robert has returned from Hotchkiss.*"

7

James Thurber

Fool, again the dream, the fancy! but I *know* my words are wild . . .

O, I see the crescent promise of my spirit hath not set;
Ancient founts of inspiration well through all my fancy yet.

. . . a long farewell to Locksley Hall!
Now for me the woods may wither, now for me the roof-tree fall.

Comes a vapor from the margin, blackening over heath and holt,
Cramming all the blast before it, in its breast a thunderbolt.

Let it fall on Locksley Hall, with rain or hail, or fire or snow;
For the mighty wind arises, roaring seaward, and I go.

"*Son, if you-all bring a gal from Calf Crick into this yere house, there's gonna be lead a-flyin' up an' down Sand Valley.*"

"*No, thank you, we're just grazing.*"

Lucius Beebe

(*with a few cutouts enabling the idle reader to dress him in the style to which he is accustomed*)

"*I just heard Herbert say 'Ergo.' That means if we don't do something we won't get out of here till two o'clock.*"

"*Take a powder, Dolan.*"

"*There's no use you trying to save me, my good man.*"

"One for you,
one for me, one for the Museum of Natural History."

"Why certainly, we've all been in one picture before."

"Now in this scene, Franz Schubert, the composer, falls asleep and dreams his melody while the girls dance it out on the piano keys. Get it?"

"I want to report a winking man."

A REVISED STATUARY
FOR THE CITY OF TOMORROW

"Why, Harriet, I hardly recognized you!"

"... so there she is, you see, sitting all by herself at the window watching this young man walk by with another girl. Then in this next picture Jane is looking pretty blue and her girl friend is saying, 'It's not that Roger doesn't still care for you, Jane. But, to be frank, no man likes to go out with a girl who never smiles; now you wouldn't be afraid to smile if you used the same kind of toothpaste as I do...'"

"...*whereas this fellow here advocates a pension of thirty dollars every day except Thursday.*"

"*Good heavens, this must be Echo Lake!*"
"*GOOD HEAVENS, THIS MUST BE ECHO LAKE!*"

"*This is the round that starts them weeping for the Spanish Loyalists.*"

William Turnesa

"For gosh sakes, here comes Mrs. Roosevelt!"

W. C. Fields

RACONTEURS

"And what do you think? Way up there at the very tippy-top of the tree was little Mr. Bobolink, singing just as if his little heart would break. And just then . . ."

*"Sure-footed
little beasts,
aren't they?"*

"Through the Tenth Dynasty to the Ming porcelain, turn right at the Italian Renaissance, and you'll see a little door."

"He advocates a doctrine of peaceful resignation."

*"And if Roosevelt is not reëlected, perhaps even a villa
in Newport, my dearest sweet."*

"*Fertig here is one of our most reliable men.*"

O. SOGLOW

"*It's all right, children. Don't even budge.*"

"*Go right on talking, please. I can't find the buzzer.*"

"We can't ask him to take it down if it's his mother."

"I think he's just stewed."

Sumner Welles

"If I told you a dream I had about you, Mr. Price, would you promise
not to do anything about it unless you really _want_ to?"

"*I'm* the one that
should be lying down somewhere."

"My husband and lover."

"Well, dear, how is it?"

"Oh, it's _you_! For a moment you gave me quite a start."

"He promised to incorporate me under
the laws of Delaware."

A REVISED STATUARY
FOR THE CITY OF TOMORROW

"Any minute now we're due for one of his
outbursts of gloomy philosophy."

Dog meat has been eaten in every major German crisis
at least since the time of Frederick the Great, and
is commonly referred to as "blockade mutton." It is

*"We must remember not to tease
our friends the wasps."*

tough, gamy, strong-flavored.
—*Time, November 25th.*

"There's a certain party I'd like to see put off the ice."

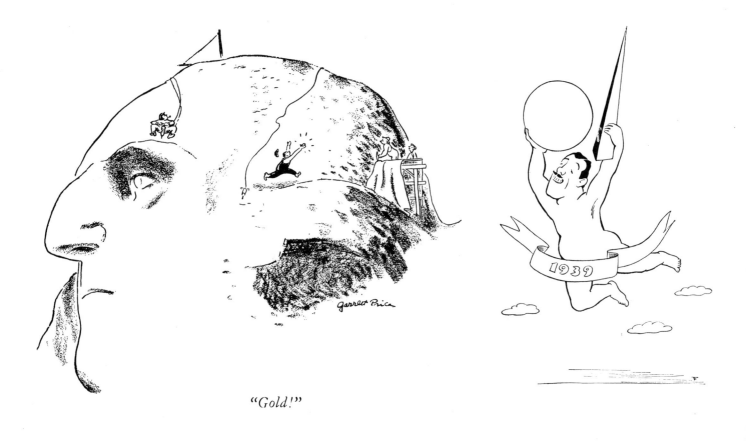

"Gold!"

"Well?"

"Well, folks, here it is starting time! . . . One moment while we take a look
at that little old schedule."

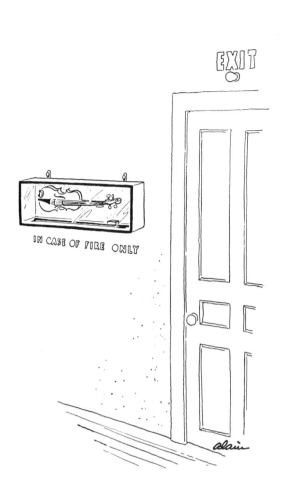

IN CASE OF FIRE ONLY

"Mr. Huntley would like to return the brooch. The young person was uncoöperative."

"I beg your pardon."

"... hold tight hold tight fooradeackasaki want some sea food Mama
shrimpers and rice they're very nice ..."

Salvador Dali

"All right, you've made the biggest hamburger
sandwich in the world. So now what?"

"Do you think we should encourage them?"

"*Darling, the doctor has discovered the nature of my allergy and I'm afraid you're in for something of a shock.*"

"*Now, there's been a lot of loose talk going around lately about splitting the atom.*"

*"My husband has insured my life
for a hundred thousand dollars. Isn't that sweet?"*

There was a young lady of Brewster
Who learned how to crow like a rooster.
On a national network
Her gift made her get work,
And the MAJOR himself introduced her!

"Gracious, George! Is that your costume?"

There's a vaporish maiden in Harrison
Who longed for the love of a Saracen,
But she had to confine her
Intent to a Shriner,
Who suffers, I fear, by comparison.

*"I couldn't get the
habeas-corpus writ,
so I brought you a saw."*

"Can't you see by now, Bernard Levin, that it's all over between us?"

"Room 707, lady in a house coat—jammed zipper."

"Now, mezzos, let me hear the thunder of hoofs!"

"Are you __still__ skeptical?"

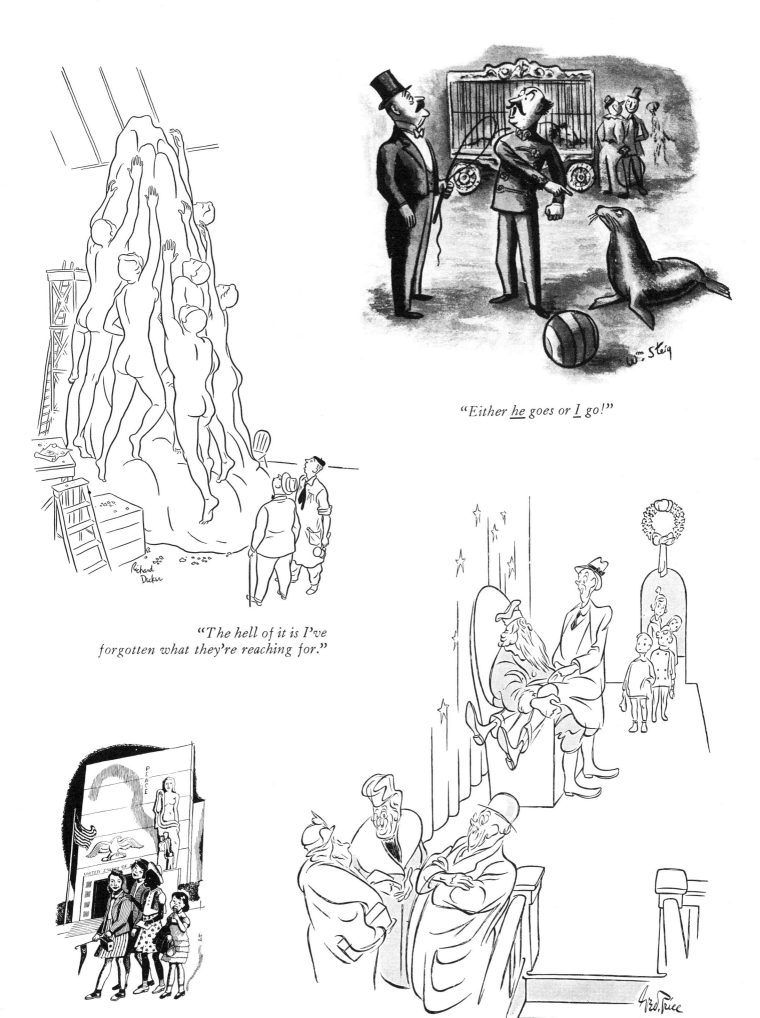

"Either _he_ goes or _I_ go!"

"The hell of it is I've
forgotten what they're reaching for."

"It's been such a struggle, but
we've managed to keep alive his belief."

RACONTEURS

"Honestly, you would have died laughing at Joe. Give him two cocktails and he thinks he's Sir Walter Raleigh or somebody. Well, when this woman at the next table drops her bag, up jumps Joe, and you know how clumsy he is anyway, and . . ."

"What have you done with Dr. Millmoss?"

Charles Spencer Chaplin

"Well, there goes Junior."

"I'm not afraid of you, Rhett Butler, or of any man in shoe leather!"

"Face the front of the car, please!"

"*Yes! we have no bananas—we have no bananas today.*"

O. SOGLOW

"And stop calling me 'Doc!'"

"Well, who *made* the magic go out of our marriage— you or me?"

"*The vote is now fifteen to one that we deplore Mussolini's attitude. I think it would be nice if we could go on record as <u>unanimously</u> deploring Mussolini's attitude.*"

"*Well—he made it!*"

"If it gives you any more trouble, let me know."

John Edgar Hoover

"No answer."

"Now look directly at me, and tell me why you haven't paid that bill I sent last September."

Frank Hague

"If *this* doesn't get us in, nothing will."

"Is it all right to take off my jacket?"

"With you I've known peace, Lida,
and now you say you're going crazy."

"*Darling, I'm sorry I called you a tramp.*"

1.

"Father, dear father, come home with me now, the clock
in the steeple strikes one. Shall I wait for an answer, sir?"

2.

3.

4.

5.

alain

*"All I know about him is
that he's apparently quite a homebody."*

...the early forties...

PRINTEMPS

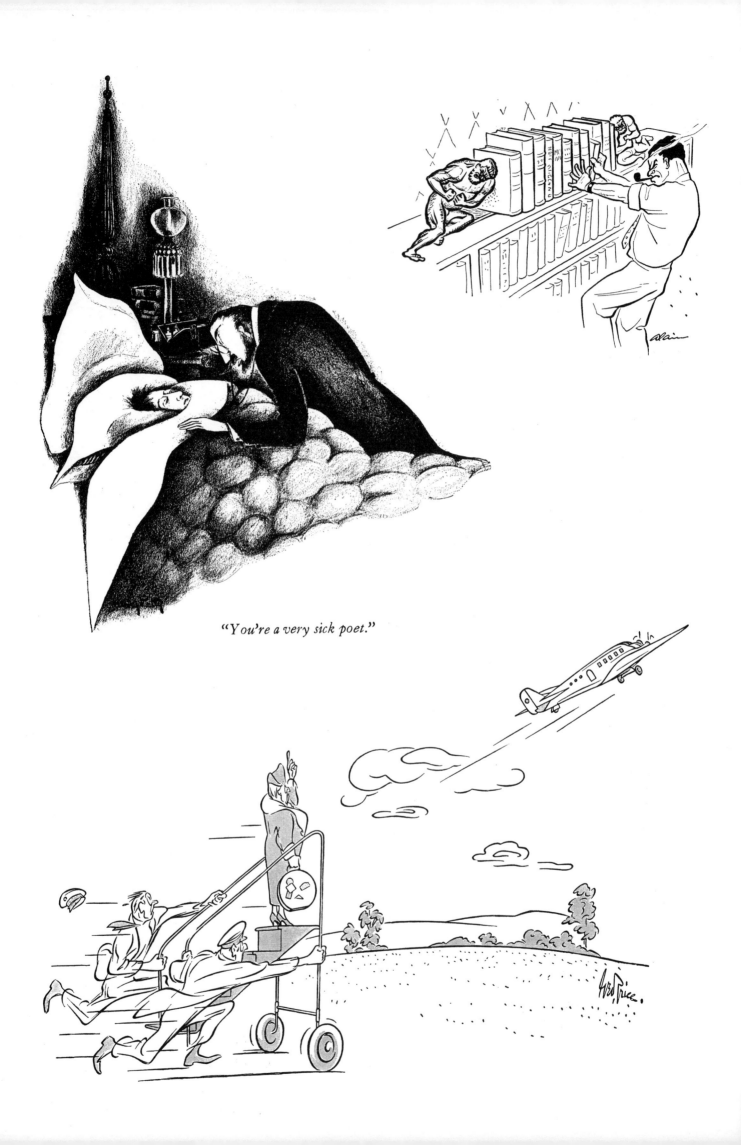

"You're a very sick poet."

"Well, if I called the wrong number, why did you answer the phone?"

"There's a fascinating legend about an Indian maiden in connection with Plots 14, 15, and most of 15A."

"And now goodbye, sir, and God bless you."

A REVISED STATUARY
FOR THE CITY OF TOMORROW

"How would you
like a little baby sister, dear?"

"These dreams of yours wherein you find great tubs
of money, Mr. Croy—can you describe the spot a
little more exactly?"

"Hey, Jack, which way to Mecca?"

"Er—ah—you are Jimmie McKinstry, aren't you?"

"And remember—the trousers to bag at the knees just ever so."

"I love the idea of there being two sexes, don't you?"

Thomas E. Dewey

"Mamma, there's a lot of people in my bed."

"And you, Streubahr . . ."

"If you don't want to look for shells, what _do_ you want to do?"

"...*the need of an experienced hand at the helm. And so let us fervently hope that the great pilot who has steered us so surely through the perilous currents of the past eight years may be prevailed upon* ..."

1

2

5

6

"If the advertising director thought it up, let the advertising director drive the damn thing!"

3

4

7

8

"PANAMA HATTIE"

This stylish brunette is Ethel Merman, about to rock the Canal Zone (and the Forty-sixth Street Theatre) with one of Cole Porter's songs. The gentleman is Arthur Treacher, playing, of all things, a butler.

"He asked me to marry him, and I evidently must have said 'Yes.'"

THE INNER MAN

Buffet Supper

Nicholas Murray Butler

"I'd like a pound of assorted cigars."

"We lack one thing, gentlemen—a motive."

"Hey, did you send my pajamas to
the laundry with my Willkie button on?"

"*I don't want to ride you, Jackson, but you're going to have to set that
old alarm clock a little earlier.*"

*"Now before we go any
further, shall we agree there's no use kidding ourselves?"*

*"Furthermore, it can be nailed, bored,
cut, or sawed—just like a plastic."*

News of destruction of Croton Aqueduct has not yet reached "Meenie." Clad in towel, she wonders why she can't draw water for her morning bubble bath. Roommate "Babs" struggles with refractory girdle, ponders rumor that Roosevelt and Cabinet have fled Washington.

Life Goes to the Collapse of Western Civilization

Pretty New York Models Get Thrilling Glimpses of Invasion and Insurrection

THESE two young girls, "Meenie" Kronkheit and "Babs" Golcz, share an apartment on Central Park South, pose for commercial photographers, like to sip Daiquiris at the Stork Club. "Babs" has been screen-tested for part of Wallace Beery's sister in forthcoming film. Both girls are good cooks, hate to wash dishes. "Babs" relaxes by walking in Central Park with "Scotty," her pet Scotty; "Meenie" by reading Gibbon's "Decline, Fall of Roman Empire." In spite of numerous dates, both showed intelligent interest in invasion of U.S. by Axis and consequent civil disturbances. LIFE's photographer spent day with them, raised skirts on still another news front of the world.

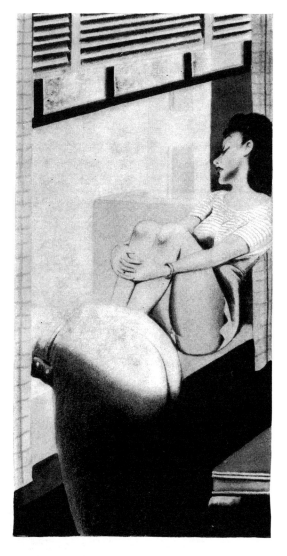

SOUND OF SCREAMS AND GUNFIRE IN STREET BELOW DRAWS "BABS" AND "MEENIE" TO APARTMENT WINDOW

VIEW FROM ROOF OF AERIAL "DOGFIGHT" INTERESTS "MEENIE," WHO HOPES SOMEDAY TO LE TO FLY HER OWN PLANE. "BABS" MUST LOSE POUND AND QUARTER BEFORE REPORTING AT ST

ographers' models and starlets have to coöperate in the shooting of "gag pictures." In this "gag ure," "Meenie" and "Babs" have dressed in scanty sports clothes for the task of lugging $3,450,000 flated United States currency to famed Elizabeth Arden's, to buy tube of vanishing cream. Ac- y, chilly October "football weather" nipped their pretty bare knees. Corpse in foreground is real.

For lark, girls take part in bread riot on upper West Side. Says "Babs": "Goodness gracious, if I ate even one slice of bread I'd have to stop wearing tailored suits." "Meenie" says she "eats like horse," never gains weight.

HILE "BABS" AND "MEENIE" EAGERLY WATCH BURNING OF MANHATTAN ISLAND AFTER BOMBING, ALERT STAFF PHOTOGRAPHER PLAYS A SLY TRICK ON THEM

CONTINUED ON NEXT PAGE

"BABS" AND "MEENIE" RIDE AS FAR AS 125TH STREET WITH REFUGEES

"Meenie" and "Babs" pose in military brothel with two lads who can't believe their luck in meeting real, live actress, model. After this picture was snapped, girls declined drinks, went home on subway. Boy friends and careers don't mix, they say.

Olsen and Johnson

"She'll be home Wednesday morning, Ma'am, but I understand she's leaving again Wednesday evening."

"Any time you want to start hoarding, Mrs. Dilley, I'd be glad to coöperate."

"Dear no, Miss Mayberry—just the head."

"*It isn't made by foot, is it?*"

"*Can they really make a Yale man a private?*"

"It's all right, Captain; I can quiet him down."

"Sometimes I get the feeling that she's trying
to tell me something."

"What do you say, everybody? Shall we dispense with
the Southern accent altogether?"

"I may be an incurable optimist,
but I _still_ think crime could be made to pay."

"A magnificent fowl, Madam. Notice how he
looks you straight in the eye."

"You said a moment ago that everybody you look at seems to be a rabbit. Now just what do you mean by that, Mrs. Sprague?"

"Somebody ought to tell him that 'poor Yorick' gag wasn't even funny the first time he pulled it."

"Occupation?"

"Woman."

"*Goodness gracious, child, what have you done?*"

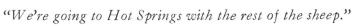

"We're going to Hot Springs with the rest of the sheep."

"At last!"

". . . and now I'm off, taking with me only the bare necessities of life."

"Of course I'm paying attention! You said you
were going to attempt to pick up the handkerchief with your teeth."

O. SOGLOW

"Watch out, Fred! Here it comes again!"

"Hear ye!
Hear ye!
I passed
English History!"

"You know the rules, Miss Wigant—no gentlemen visitors after ten P.M."

"Margaret, is there a moon?"

Anna Rosenberg

SMALL FRY

Hesitant Diver

"Congratulations! It's a baby."

*"When you say that I'm sound as
a dollar, Doctor, just what do you mean?"*

"No thank you. I don't drink."

"I said no, and I mean no."

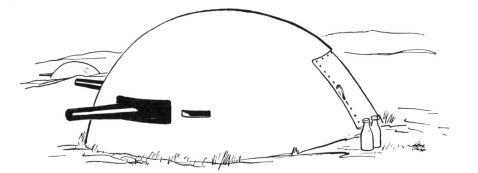

"Is that a twitch, Madam,
or are you giving me the old come-on?"

"Please, Martin, can't
you lean somewhere else?"

"Oh, *that's* Herbert's muse."

"George, guess what! I'm starting a swimming pool."

"Mother, I'd like you to meet a member
of the armed forces."

"Why do you keep raising me when you _know_ I'm bluffing?"

Alfred Gwynne Vanderbilt

"Tell me more about your husband, Mrs. Briggs."

"Look at it this way—you're the baby sparrow and I'm the mamma sparrow."

"By George, I wish I'd said that!"

"How old is a Major?"

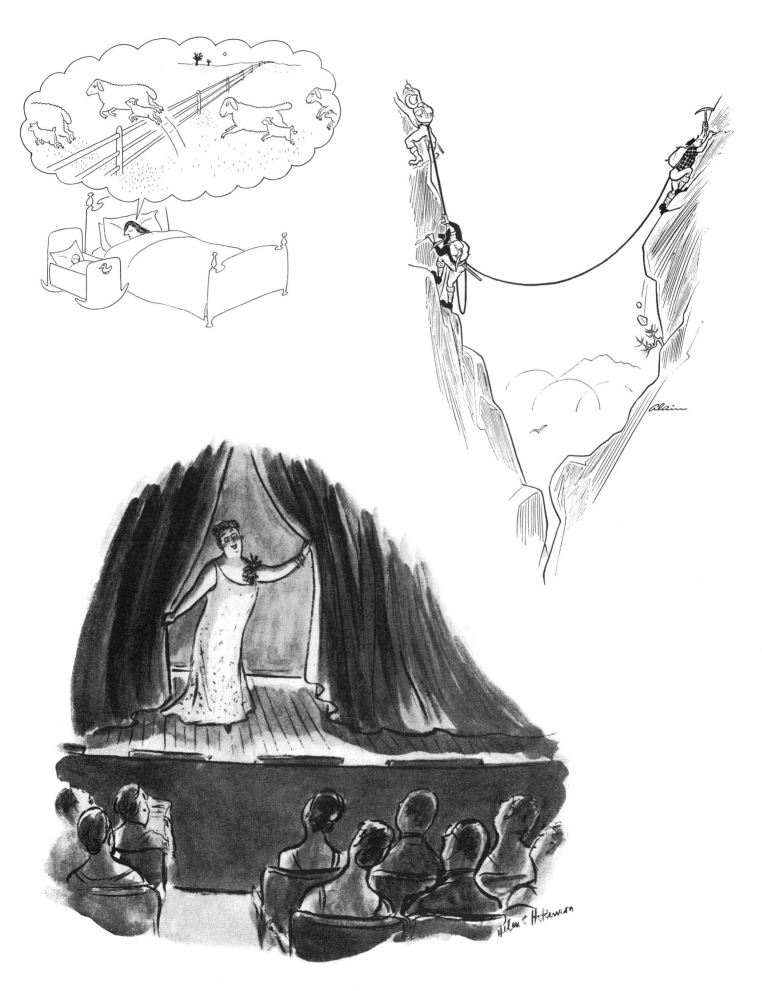

"Enough of Prologue! Now let's have the play.
"'The Pageant of Distinguished Bergen County Women' is under way."

"*The one I'm with is certainly a cluck. He don't know where he's been, or where he's going, or anything.*"

"Pop, can I have the elephant tonight?"

"Catty-corners . . . march!"

"No, I don't want to sell my vacuum cleaner."

"Don't feel bad, Nelson. With normal growth, you'll be in there next year."

"Makes quite a ceremony out of those draft notices, doesn't he?"

"Paramount News sends its respects, sir, and could we move a little closer to the atoll?"

"Now, of course Antony and Cleopatra were very dear friends."

Le Corbusier

"We don't sell them singly, Madam. It breaks up the formation."

"You got him worried
now. He's afraid he'll kill you."

Tact is one of your virtues. You meet people
well and revel in witty conversation. Why not
cultivate an interest in art? Too much emphasis
on business matters is the one thing you should
guard against. Your interest in the opposite sex
makes you in great demand as a dinner partner.

"It's been taken care of."

"Ah, Miss Bergdall, your headache seems much better!"

"Gabriel Heatter was every bit as surprised as I was."

"Of course, if __he__ leaves for a defense job we're licked."

Newbold Morris

"*Martha, my secretary doesn't understand me.*"

"*. . . and don't call me Mac!*"

"I can't decide whether to quit right there and call it 'Woman' or go on and make it look like a woman."

"They're friends—leftovers from the old Dale Carnegie days."

"It's marvellous! All you do is add water."

"And how does everybody want their eggs _this_ morning?"

"Strike him out."

STEINBERG

"And hereafter if there's anything you don't like, come to me—don't write to Mrs. Roosevelt."

Willie Hoppe

"Well, that's show business."

"*And now, friends, we put aside frivolity for a moment and present our new feature number, the Arsenal of Democracy.*"

THE WRITING PUBLIC

"Dear Fred:—Saw you folks going out to the movies tonight, and just thought I'd slip a note under your door before I forgot. Just wanted to say that it's been a long time since we had a game of bridge with you folks. We must try to get together soon. By the way, just happened to notice this morning that your dog has been digging in our flower beds. No great harm done, of course, but we were just wondering if . . ."

"I think I may say, without fear of contradiction . . .

"Hello, paleface!"

"I suppose to him I'm some sort of god."

"Yeah?"
"Yeah!"

"Any children?"

"Lots of little men have got somewhere—Napoleon, Dollfuss, Billy Rose."

"Well, that's how it is, men. You just rub two dry sticks together."

"Just tell her a
Hollywood scout is here to see her."

"Can we be ready in ten minutes?"

"Ouch, sir!"

"*Albert, I did something wrong on the George Washington Bridge.*"

"*I tell you, Mamma, the blood keeps going to my head.*"

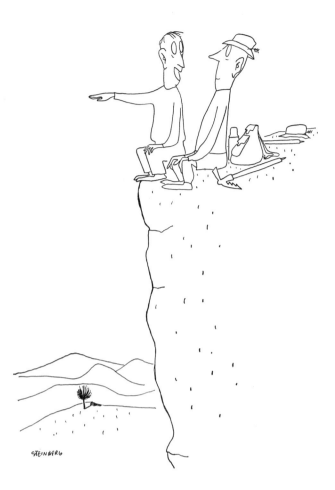

"You'd hardly know my Tommy. He's about that tall now."

"Of course, you'll have to be on the qui vive during blackouts."

"Quicksand or not, Barclay, I've half a mind to struggle."

"... and never, never go near a house with a well-beaten path to the door."

"All right. Now, this time you be the speeder and I'll be the cop."

Percy Grainger

"Cut it, Dolan! Remember we're in uniform."

"*Is it O.K., Joe, to refer to our subscribers as readers?*"

"*If she could only cook!*"

"*Are you sure you <u>wore</u> a hat?*"

"Oh, I don't know—
I just feel sort of _out_ of things."

"Daddy's gone back to camp, Helen is at the canteen, Bill's at a troop meeting, and Mother's still at the plant. Is there anything _I_ can do for you?"

"Still, did you ever stop to think where you and I would be if it _weren't_ for evil?"

NO PARKING, MADAME

TWEEDS

"Which helps Great Britain the most—tweeds or whiskey?"

"Boy, did _I_ have an afternoon! The census man was here."

1.

2.

"Perhaps we didn't make it clear, Miss Jones, that your job with the F.B.I. is purely clerical."

3.

"No, no, McNamara. Just that white fluffy stuff on top."

"I just got damn well fed up with being formal all the time."

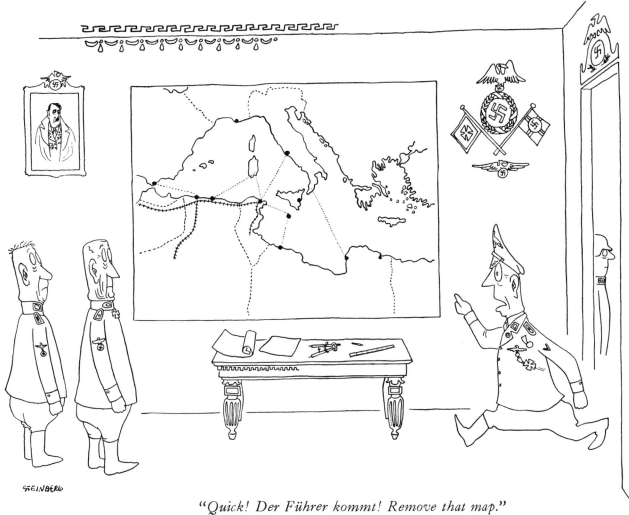

"Quick! Der Führer kommt! Remove that map."

"I'm calling it 'Girl Without a Dirndl.'"

"I see Aubrey Arden is getting married for the fourth time. That would be a sweet account to have."

'What I'm _really_ looking for is some little investment that won't keep bobbing up and down."

"*Au secours! Sauvez-moi! Au secours!*"

STEINBERG

"*If he's not a Frenchman he's certainly an awful snob.*"

"*You ask him for gas if you want to. I'd rather die first!*"

Lily Pons

"Do you realize that another
Christmas is practically at our throats?"

"I'm telling you for the
last time—keep the hell off this corner!"

"Is this seat taken?"

STEINBERG

"Watch it, Charlotte, you're tending to lead again."

"Do me one favor, will you—stop saying 'entre nous.'"

"Hold it, Lucy! Here I am."

"Oh, speak up, George! Stop mumbling!"

"... and then I covered them
with dirt, and that was the last I ever saw of them."

"Professor Caswell tells me this damn thing happens to be a Ubangi symbol of fertility."

"I don't go for this long-hair stuff."

"One single."

Harry L. Hopkins

"I realize this is like carrying coals to Newcastle."

"Just walk around and mingle. Don't drink more than two—just enough to show you're a good sport. Don't show that you're shocked by anything the ladies say. Stay around about half an hour and then go home."

"It's the Times' bulletins every hour on the hour, the Daily News' bulletins every hour on the half-hour, and those damn carrier pigeons in between."

"*Elizabeth Conner McMeekin, '15?*"

"*Present. After graduation, I started to take an M.A. at Teachers College, but gave it up to marry Roy McMeekin, Cornell, '12. My husband was only a plant engineer with the telephone company at the time and had not yet become an executive. We lived in Columbus, Ohio, until 1927, when Mr. McMeekin was called to New York, and we built a home in Westchester. I have two children, a girl, Elsie, aged nineteen, and a boy, Donald, aged seventeen. I want to say that I think this Alpha Delta Alpha alumnae picnic is a wonderful idea and that Penny Trowbridge should be congratulated on getting it up. I hope we can get together next summer and repeat it with all the same people.*"

"I'm sorry. This section is reserved for officers."

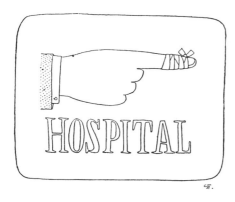

"Now this, children, is what we call a bird's-eye view."

"I don't believe I care for anything, thank you. I'm just in their car pool."

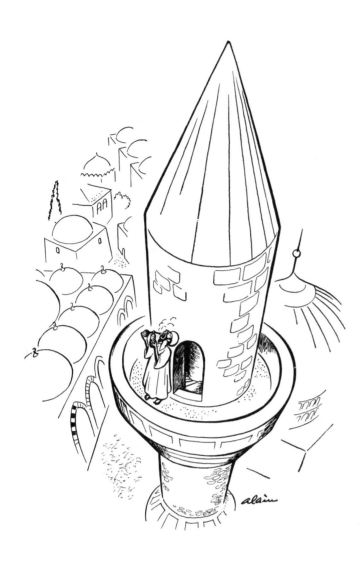

"And now I want to thank you very much."

"For heaven's sake, stop worrying. You're _supposed_ to feel sluggish!"

DREAMS OF GLORY

"There! Now you're getting the hang of it."

"My light is _not_
showing, and get off my tulip bed!"

4. THANK GOD FOR THE INVASION!

"Watch out for that Rogers girl. She has lint."

"*Corporal Thomas E. Harrison writes from the southwest Pacific, 'Thank you all for your round-robin letter. It sure was interesting and I sure was surprised to get it. Goodbye now.' Private First Class Roland V. Brill writes from somewhere in Alaska, 'Well, it certainly was a big surprise . . .'*"

"*No. 33. The—er—Baseball Player!*"

"Ask Marshall! Ask Eisenhower! How should *I* know why it was rejected?"

". . . and this one is for Coca-Cola."

"She's bankrupt in every way except financially."

"You're *speaking* to B. J. Wetherby, dammit!"

"Stop 'Madaming' me!"

"Insist on Pasfo! Remember that when you drop the first letter and interchange the next two, simultaneously substituting an 'e' for the final 'o,' it spells 'SAFE.' Yes, Pasfo is the safe way to counteract the annoying discomfort that so often accompanies the common head cold."

"Imagine! Right in the middle of our Greater East Asia Co-Prosperity Sphere!"

"*I lost interest in this
one. I figured what the hell, just another nude.*"

"*Agnes called to say that dear old Mrs. Pulsifer
passed away at ten this morning and that maybe
we could get her apartment.*"

"What I can't understand—why doesn't everyone just keep doubling their bets?"

"I llove you."

THE READING PUBLIC

"Another case finished, another poor, misguided devil who will pay for his crimes on the gallows." Inspector Trunnel leaned back comfortably, crossed his tweed-clad legs, and dipped his pipe into his tobacco pouch.

"I'm afraid I'm most awfully dense, but I still don't see how you worked it out," I said, pushing the decanter toward him. "Why, I thought Gruber had the best alibi of the whole lot."

"That's just it, my boy," said Trunnel. "He had too good an alibi. Mark you, Sheila Trent-Quayle said she saw him in the yew alley before ten forty-three, when she retired. Of course, we now know that she was covering up for young Lovering, who she feared was implicated. But if Gruber didn't go to the stables before eleven-three, and if the butler didn't set out the tray of sandwiches until eleven-fifteen, that scene in the billiard room between Gruber and Blaylock couldn't have taken place before midnight. Here, let me just draw up a timetable . . ."

FOURTEENTH AIR FORCE
CHINA THEATRE

No mail

Taxi

Flying in

"I can see it all now. Bands playing! Our boys marching up the Avenue! Cheering throngs and people throwing paper from every window! Oh, it'll be perfect hell."

"Right after church we're going to try hot buttered rum made with oleo."

"See what I mean, men? Now, when the next alarm comes in, I hope there'll be less dawdling."

"I got a waterproof, shockproof, rustproof, non-magnetic watch, but I lost it."

"Practically all my calls come from the 'National Geographic.'"

"*I think of you as being enormously alive.*"

"*Like this—see? You've got to get your back into it.*"

"*One belief is that every person is inhabited by a spirit, or ko, which goes travelling while the human body is asleep. If a man should be awakened suddenly—so the belief is— the ko might not have time to get back into its body and would get even by going around causing trouble. So the people believe a man should be allowed to sleep until he wakes up of his own accord.*"—U.S. Army Pocket Guide to New Caledonia.

"*Professor Merton is a brilliant man in his field, but he has absolutely no small talk.*"

"*. . . and then I came into possession of certain monies which the State alleged belonged to the First National Bank.*"

"*. . . and in conclusion, Mr. President, I say that if after this great war we are to have a federation of all nations of the earth, where would it be more fitting to have the seat of government of this great brotherhood of free and friendly peoples than right here in God's country?*"

"*Frankly, I don't take much stock in this business of the gods being angry. The way I got it doped out is that at great depths the heat caused by the enormous pressure of the earth's crust melts the stone and turns some of it into gases. See? Then you got down there a vapor tension strong enough to blow the whole works to the surface, providing, of course, a channel of weakness opens up for it.*"

"Gracious! I certainly _am_ at the wrong window!"

"Pardon me, but have you seen anything of a five-gaited horse?"

"But you just had a drink last week!"

"Now, now, Miss Van Voorhis. Let's not put the cart before the horse."

"Everyone has money these days."

"Now you and I are going to share a little secret."

"What has eyes and can't see?"

"No, Madam, it's not our special for today. It's what we got."

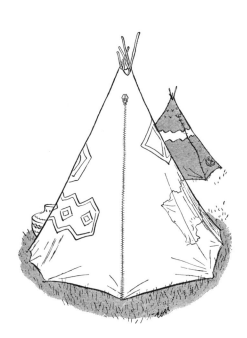

"He's a big fellow, that Grogan, isn't he?"

"Amazingly faithful clientele, isn't it?"

"*Which one is the love potion?*"

"*Of course, we could adopt some.*"

"Zey call me Muzzer Goddam."

"Wherever Hartwell goes, he tries to make at least one new friend."

"Whoa! Damn it, whoa!"

"Chef is making out the menu for the day. Would you mind telling me how you spell your name?"

"Gee, Jack! That was very careless of you."

"Well, back to the old drawing board."

"*Vos yeux sont comme des étoiles, vos cheveux des tresses d'or, votre bouche est un frais bouton de rose; comme vous êtes belle, ma chérie, et comme vous êtes adorable...*"

THE OLDEN TIME

The Dragon

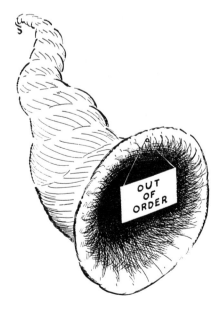

"*When you speak of better times, Hubert, do you mean when the war is over or when the Democrats are over?*"

"*That's war. We bomb Washington, they bomb Tokio.*"

"Good heavens! Am I supposed to see this?"

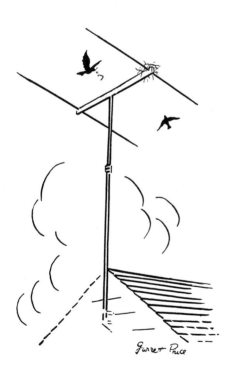

"Here is a summary of the programs you will hear over this station immediately following this announcement. At twelve-fifteen, 'Big Sister;' at twelve-thirty, 'The Story of Helen Trent;' 'Life Can Be Beautiful' comes on at one and 'Ma Perkins' at one-fifteen; 'Young Doctor Malone' is presented at one-thirty, followed fifteen minutes later by 'Road of Life' . . ."

"When were you built?"

Omar N. Bradley

*"To put my problem to you frankly, Mr. Anthony, my
husband threatens to leave me if I tune in your program once more."*

P Barlow

"I want to report a helicopter."

"I just thought I'd stop in
and tell you that the luncheon was a *huge* success."

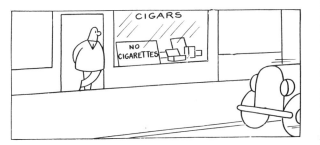

"It was lent anonymously."
"Well, I should *think* so!"

Dr. Gallup

"The papers are all in that
tin box, there won't be any
trouble about the insurance,
and anything you don't
understand, ask the lawyer."

"Suddenly he was no longer the man I loved. It was as if I were shooting a total stranger."

"Then right here you start worrying are you maybe going nuts."

...the late forties...

"Oh, dear, I'd really be enjoying all this if it weren't for Russia."

"Oh, I'm not waiting for anyone in particular."

"We'll have to stop seeing each other, Evelyn. She's getting wise to what happened to the Luftwaffe."

"*You and your 'just one more tap'!*"

1

2

3

4

5

6

7

8

9

10

11

12

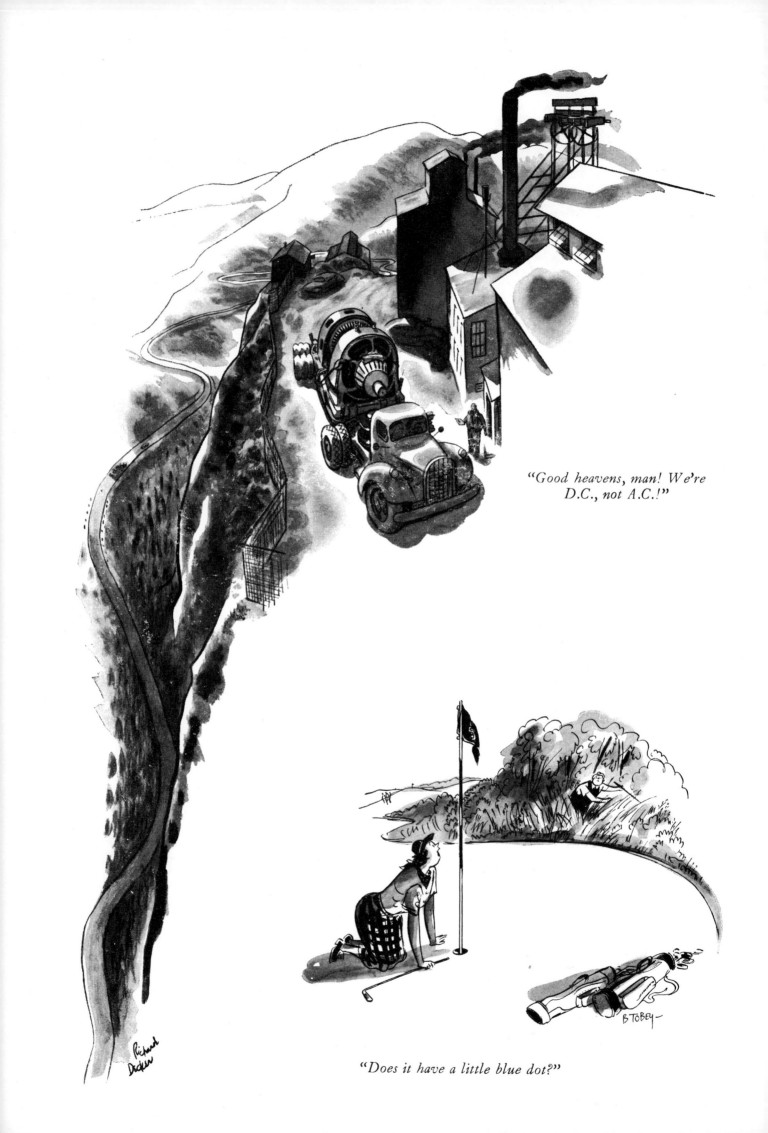

"Good heavens, man! We're
D.C., not A.C.!"

"Does it have a little blue dot?"

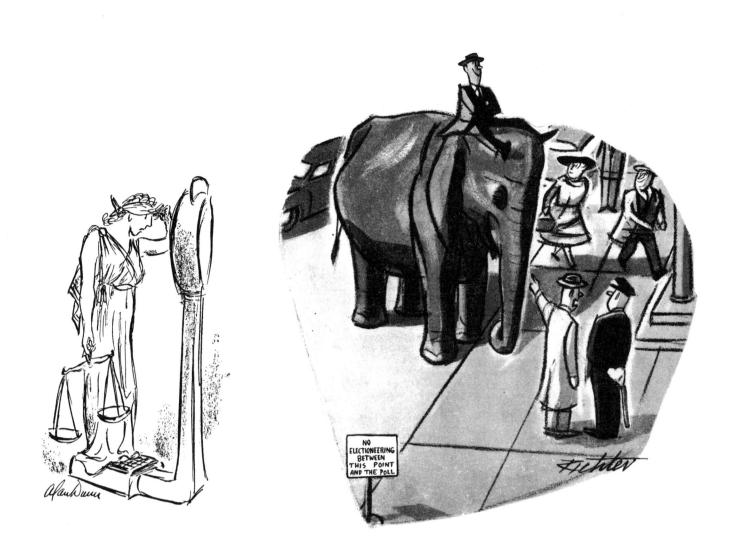

"*And I say he is electioneering!*"

EVERYDAY HISTRIONICS

The poet at the picnic

"You always said you could lick
him with your eyes closed. Now's your chance."

"Karl Marx say . . ."

"Why don't *we* ever have potato pancakes?"

"That's Mr. Anderson, but I don't think that's <u>Mrs.</u> Anderson."

"*In the interests of science, Miss Mellish, I'm going to make a rather strange request of you.*"

3

4

"With you, it's different. You've got talent,
courage, imagination, savoir-faire . . ."

"Yoohoo, Justice! How late are you open?"

"Hello, Larry. You know everyone, I suppose?"

"Hand me that bottle of all-purpose sherry."

"*Dearest: How I wish you were here with me now to see how lovely our little garden has become! The black nightshade is in full bloom, and the death camass we planted last fall is coming along beautifully. The henbane seems to have shot up overnight. You will be glad to know that the dwarf's hair was not affected by the dry spell, as we feared, after all. A myriad delightful little slugs have appeared, as if from nowhere, on the rotten stump by the belladonna patch, and this morning I noticed snake eggs hatching near the pool. Do finish up that business, darling, and hurry home.*"

"There! How do you like being splashed?"

"We find the defendant very, very guilty."

"It's the most disheartening case of backsliding I've ever seen."

"I can tell you one thing right off—you can't solve your problems by running away."

"Macy's is closed!"

"I like your looks, Ramsey. You're hired."

"It's good to hear _yours_, too."

"Goodness, Mr. Harrison, seventy-eight isn't old!"

1

2

3

4

5

"My parents taught me to fear God and respect my fellow-man. I was president of my class at college and was voted most likely to succeed. After graduation, I joined the staff of a large corporation and devoted all my energy to my work. I neither drank nor smoked nor let pleasure deflect me from my objective. As the years passed, my devotion was rewarded with increasing responsibilities until finally I was elected Chairman of the Board. I was given an honorary degree by Columbia, and the President of the United States bestowed on me the Medal of Merit for services in my country's behalf. At the height of my career, I was invited to pose for an advertisement featuring men of outstanding accomplishment. I accepted this honor. The photographer posed me before his camera and placed in my hand a glass of liquid. Out of curiosity, I took a sip—and then another sip—an another . . ."

"Truman it does something for. You it doesn't."

"Know any more short cuts?"

"Suppose he doesn't get the best marks
in his class. Do you get the highest salary in your office?"

"You sure had your nerve to tell a sergeant off
like that. What did _he_ say?"

"O.K., Charlie. This is the place."

"If the next one passes us by, we better split up."

"It's awfully kind of you, but I'm trying to give up smoking."

"Oh, darling, can you step out for a moment?"

"I go to all the trouble of driving these anemones from Babylon, and what do they do? They hang their heads!"

"If we get separated, look for me in the cyclamens."

"Do you really think it's playing fair to shellac a pussy willow?"

GARDEN CLUB of AMERICA

"I'm terribly nervous. In just a few minutes, I'm going to be judged by Mrs. C. Monford Cole."

"Calendula . . . snapdragon . . . chicken wire . . . nippers . . ."

"I want to achieve the effect
of a sombrero carelessly thrown down."

"But we can't go back
to the Waldorf with a _rake_!"

1

2

3

4

5

6

*"What gets me is why they made all their
buildings look like banks."*

"*You're a mystic, Mr. Ryan. All Irishmen are mystics.*"

7

8

"They'd make a cute couple, except for her."

Bobby Clark

"Save your breath, Betty-Lou."

"It's the children, darling—back from camp."

"You remember two years ago, Corwin, when you said that if I didn't like your work, I knew what I could do?"

"Well, then, how about _Friday_ evening?"

"...and, furthermore, I give you my solemn promise that if I am elected, I'll pay off every debt I owe in this town, one hundred cents on the dollar."

"Vous n'avez pas un sou pour une tasse de café?"

"Then I says to him, 'To hell wit' you, Tom Brady!'"

"Papa doesn't know _everything_, son."

"No, you've got the right number. It's just that I'm not sitting any more."

"Why, no, I didn't see any fox go past here."

"Well, mine got off to an even slower start than yours
—a few reviews buried in the Sunday book supple-
ments, hardly enough to provide blurbs for the ads,
and a squib in the 'Saturday Review.' Then Jinx and
Tex had me for breakfast one morning, and before I
knew what had happened, Mary Margaret McBride
was on the phone, Ess and Ess had appropriated ten
thousand more for publicity, and my agent shot me
through the Middle West on an autographing tour.
Now I'm right smack on the best-seller list."

"When I was your age, you was a baby already."

"I just want to say that I'm perfectly willing to serve as treasurer, provided
every penny doesn't have to come out exactly even."

1.

2.

"Charlie! Please! Not here!"

3.

4.

5.

6.

"You are charged with disorderly
conduct, indecent exposure, and impersonating an officer."

*"Look at 'em out there! I'd like
to see my wife dragging me to this kind of a thing!"*

"For Heaven's sake, why don't you go outdoors and trace something?"

"Say, how about _us_ having sort of an office party?"

"Who they _should_ have in there is that Mr. Bates in Accounting."

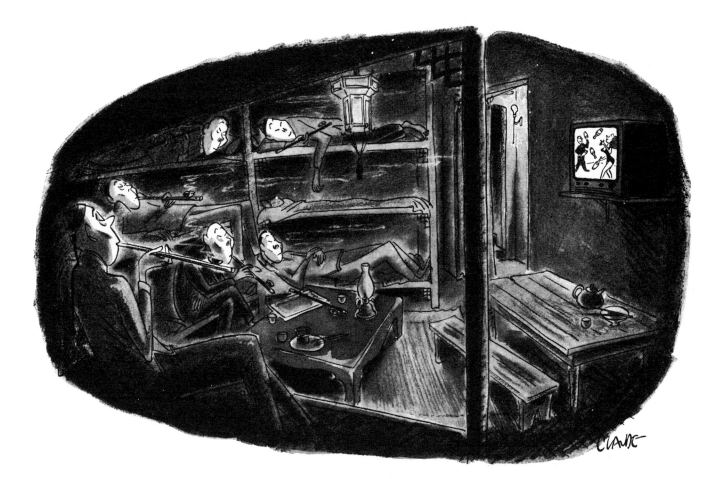

"I'd like to see them wriggle out of this. I bought a ticket on every horse in the race."

"If _we_ invented this damn thing, why can't we make it work?"

"What a silly place to plant a tree!"

cobean

AMERICA'S PLAYGROUNDS

Provincetown

"... and meanwhile, we, the great middle class, are being slowly crushed between the upper and the nether millstones."

"When my husband sees how much I've bought, he'll throw me right out of the house."

"... you, Spade—you're moving too fast, and you're looking back over your shoulder. You're nervous, Pete, nervous. You nosed the car in much too sharply, and you parked too far from the corner. You're lucky another heap didn't move in ahead of you and bottle you up. Watch that. Lefty, you were supposed to be covering for cops ..."

2

"Really? Why, I'm from Vermont myself."

"Hmm—I don't like the looks of that eye."

"I must be doing all right. Mr. Curtis made a pass at me today."

"I understand old Burton decided you *can* take it with you."

"Fill 'er up."

"We want the button made
of some tough, permanent material."

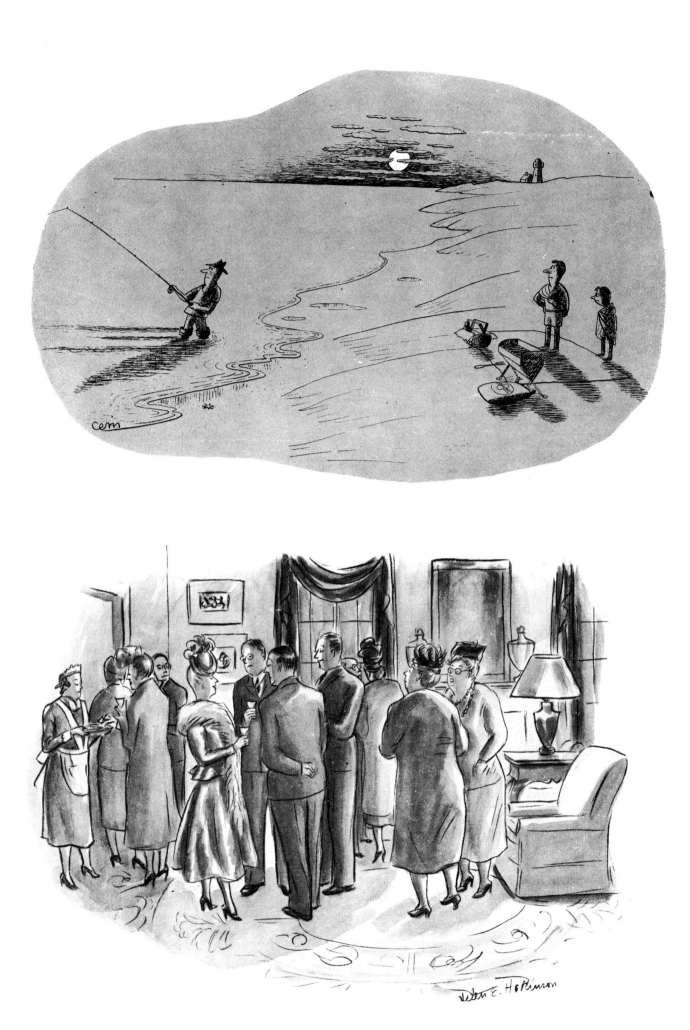

"Personally, I wouldn't want husband after husband after husband."

"When you say you hate your
species, Ronald, do you mean *everyone*?"

"*Harris, I've cancelled your hospitalization and sick-benefit policy, closed out your old-age retirement account, cleared your case with the union, given proper legal notice to the Unemployment Insurance Bureau, and had a check drawn for your vacation credit, cost-of-living bonus, severance pay, and accumulated salary, including overtime. You're fired!*"

"*You're going to marry a tall, dark couple.*"

"*Well, Mr. Favorite Nephew!*"

"The scene is a typical stodgy suburban living room. The wallpaper would leave no impression on you because you've seen the pattern a thousand times. There is the inevitable wing-back chair, covered, as you might know, in flowered chintz, with a shirred flounce; a ship on the mantel; a whatnot in the corner; and a lamp with a parchment shade. . . ."

"*George! George! Drop the keys!*"

"*Why doesn't he pick on his own sex for a change?*"

"*I'm just local sustaining now, but the theory is that I'm network potential.*"

"You know, sometimes I can't help wondering if Mr. Lawrence
really *did* go to South America."

"*John Hawkins! You know perfectly well you
lost that compass on purpose.*"

"*Well, he's five feet three, weighs about a hundred and ten, hair very thin, has watery eyes, a squint, and a kind of scraggly mustache, wears horn-rimmed glasses, and—uh—oh, the hell with it. Never mind.*"

"Want to sit on this side, Lefty?"

"I never thought _that_
kind of people were Republicans."

DREAMS OF GLORY

Pearl Diver

1

2

3

4

"*Notice the little ruffle, which gives it that feminine touch.*"

5

6

Trygve Lie

"Do you remember, Crosby, when the only thing to fear was fear itself?"

"Like that?"

"I'm Mrs. Chester Frye and this is my friend Mrs. Goodly. We're from Manhasset, Long Island, and, frankly, we're just a pair of old snoops."

"Take away the décolletage, and what have you got?"

"Harold! You promised!"

"Well, what'll we do today?"

2

3

4

"Do you need money? If it's ready cash you want—
no delay, no red tape—then come at once to . . .

. . . the Happy Days Loan Company. Write down the address . . ."

5

6

7

*" . . . and as you leave these tranquil, ivied walls to face
the stern realities of life . . . "*

"Here's the record, Chief. He's a member of the Sons of Democracy, the American Friends of Worldwide Democracy, the Guardians of the American Heritage, the People's League for Good Citizenship, the Friends of Freedom, the Conference for the Furtherance of Constitutional Government, the League for the Preservation of American Freedom, the Sentinels of Democracy, the Golden Rule Association, the Society for the Support of the Constitution of the United States, the International Congress for the Furtherance of Democracy, the Conference for the Observance of the Ten Commandments, and the Society for the Preservation of North American Wild Life. We think he's a Commie."

"Is your—ah—mate in?"

"All right, Joe, you can knock off."

"You *couldn't* have been listening. If you'd been listening, you'd be mad."

"*Blanco Pasta's full of juice,*
Just the thing for daily use;
Two full servings, cold or hot,
For ten lire—that's a lot!
Vitamins are added, too.
Blanco's is the buy for you!"

"*Now, George—you __promised__!*"

"She's very like her father and has something
of his sense of humor."

"What gets me is that having to love everybody
whether you like them or not."

"I happen to be a MacNab, Miss. I couldn't help noticing that you're wearing our tartan."

"...and on the left, wearing purple tights—Giovanni Maricini."

"But *we* couldn't have a modern house! Oh, no! Modern was too extreme for *us*!"

"I sometimes wonder about Brother Bartholomew."

"I hate to see de evenin' sun go down . . ."

"*This is the big one, folks. . . . Now he's sighting the putt. . . . Now he's bending over and addressing the ball. . . . Now he's glaring in my direction . . .*"

"*I didn't say anything. That was yesterday.*"

"Albert, how big a standing army do you suppose we'd have to have to stay at peace with the *whole* world?"

"Good morning, Reilly! Here I am."

"And now, just before the next depression I want you to take all my money out of stocks and buy bonds."

Special
NECKLACES
FORMERLY $2 50
NOW ONLY $6 00

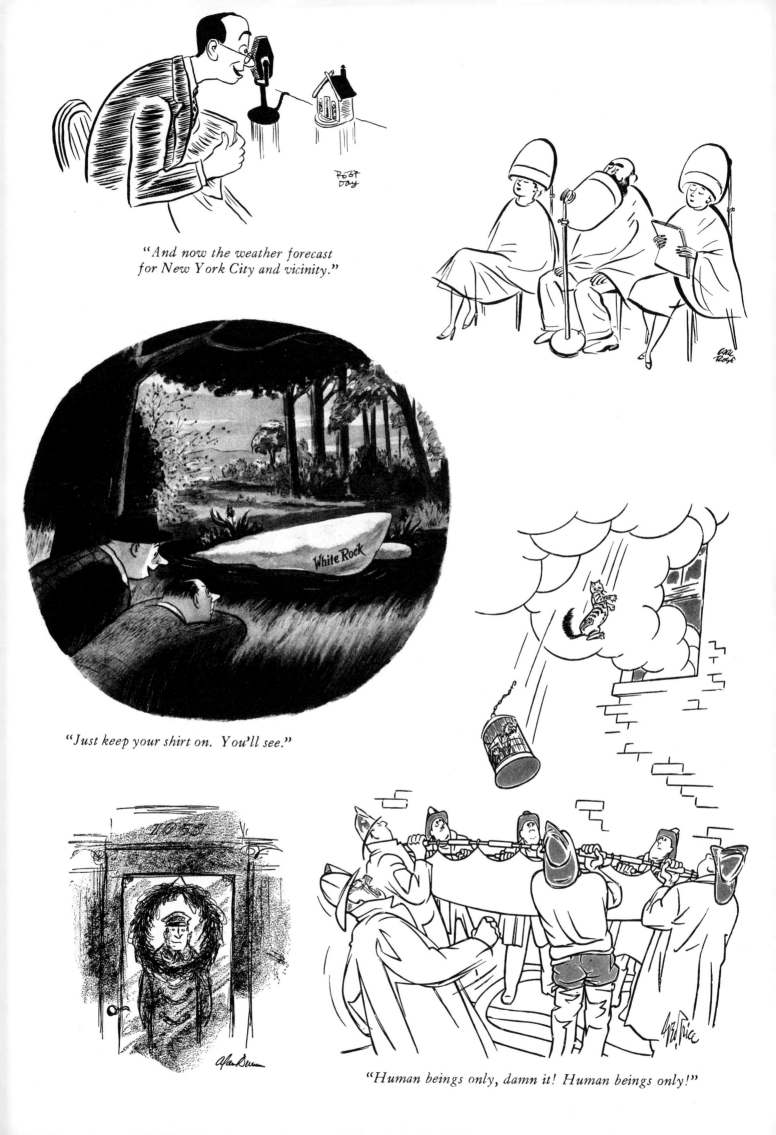

"And now the weather forecast for New York City and vicinity."

"Just keep your shirt on. You'll see."

"Human beings only, damn it! Human beings only!"

"I can lick any woman in the house!"

"On the contrary, I think
they make you look very distinguished."

"Talk about argument, cajolery, threats!"

"Mr. Kirby says there's no such thing as smoked oysters."